APJ Abdul Kalam —The Missile Man of India

Dr. APJ Abdul Kalam is one of the most distinguished scientist of India. He is a renowned professor, aeronautical engineer and the chancellor of the Indian Institute of Space Science and Technology (IIST).

Dr. APJ Abdul Kalam served as the 11th President of India from 2002 to 2007. He is often referred as 'People's President'. He is also popularly known as the 'Missile Man of India', because of his extraordinary contribution in the development of Ballistic Missile project and Space Rocket Technology. He also worked as a scientist in ISRO and DRDO. He was awarded with the Bharat Ratna—India's highest civilian honour in 1997.

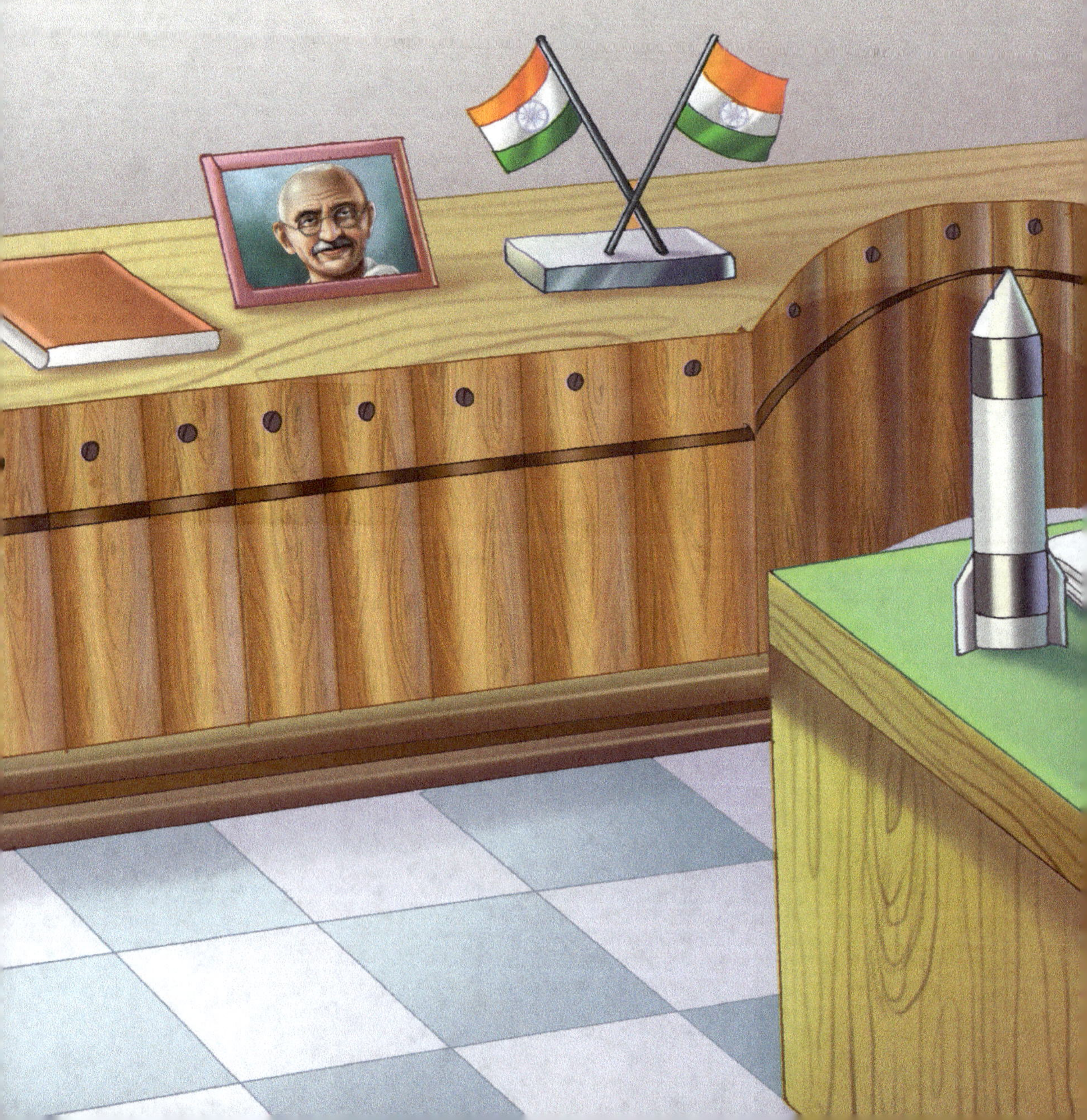

Birth and Early Years of Dr. Kalam's Life

Dr. APJ Abdul Kalam was born in Rameshwaram (in Tamilnadu) in a middle-class Muslim family on 15th October 1931. His father was Jainulabdeen and mother was Ashiamma. Dr. Kalam's full name is Avul Pakir Jainulabdeen. His father was a devout Muslim, who had good relations with the Rameshwaram temple priests. He used to rent his owned boats out to the local fishermen. He was a good friend of the Hindu religious leaders and school teachers of Rameshwaram.

During his childhood, Dr. Kalam lived very close to the sea. He developed a great passion for nature and sea. He used to spend a lot of time watching the waves of sea. His mother influenced him to a great extent in developing his talents in music and writing poetry.

Dr. Kalam's parents led a very simple lifestyle. They imbibed good moral values in their children. Dr. Kalam became religious at a very young age. He reads 'Quran' and 'Bhagwat Geeta' daily and strictly follows vegetarian diet. Dr. Kalam devoted his entire life in doing research work.

Dr. Kalam spent most of his childhood in financial problems. His education began in a rural primary school at Rameshwaram. Later, he was shifted to Ramnathpuram Missionary School.

Dr. Kalam started working at a very early age. To bear the expenses of his education, he worked as a newspaper hawker.

His teachers, parents and others noticed his efforts and brilliance. Some of his teachers even came forward to help him.

After completing his school education in 1954, he took his graduation degree in Physics from St. Joseph College, Tiruchirapalli. In 1957, Kalam completed Bachelor of Engg. in Aerospace engineering from Madras Institute of Technology. Later he obtained advanced master and doctorate degrees in his respected field from the same institute.

Dr. Kalam's Professional Life

After completing his third year at MIT, he joined Hindustan Aeronautics Limited (HAL), Bangalore as a trainee and worked on the piston and turbine engines. In 1958, he came out of Hindustan Aeronautics Limited as a graduate.

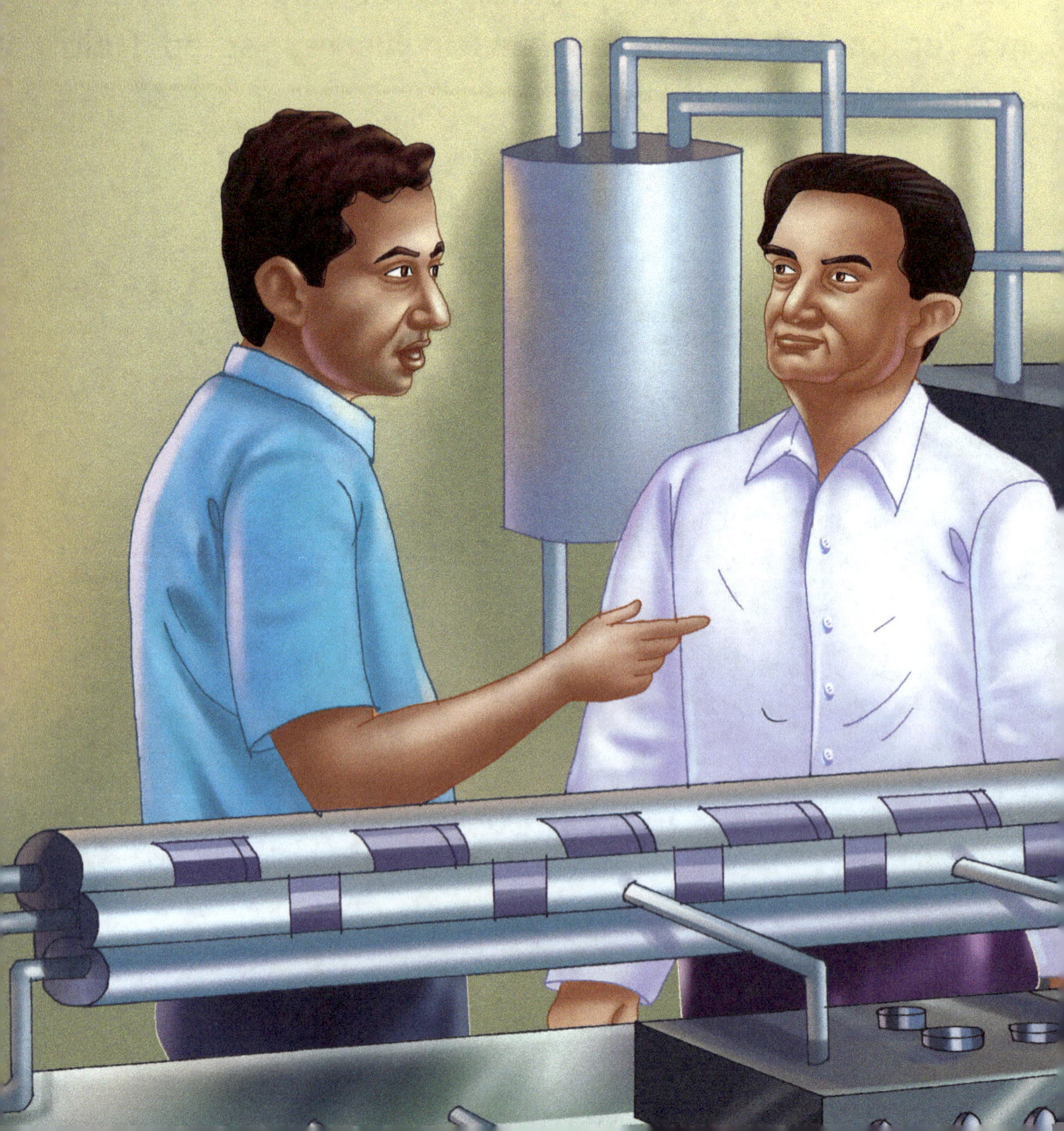

Thereafter, he got the opportunity to sewed at Indian Space Research Organisation (ISRO). After working on the several projects, he soon became a Project Director for India's first indigenous satellite launch vehicle (SLV-III) at Thumba.

The SLV-3 project was successful in placing Rohini—a scientific satellite—into orbit in July 1980 and was honoured with a Padma Bhushan in 1981. During this time, Dr. Kalam got to work with three great minds—Dr. Vikram Sarabhai, Professor Satish Dhawan and Dr. Brahm Prakash. He has also acknowledged these three people in his autobiography.

The second phase of Dr. Kalam's professional life started when he joined Defence Research Development Organisation (DRDO) in 1982. As Director of DRDO, he was entrusted with Integrated Guided Missile Development Program (IGMDP).

He played a major role in the development of many important Missiles like Nag, Akash, Trishul, Agni and Prithvi.

Three new laboratories for missile technologies were also developed during his tenure. His contributions in India's defence system are admirable.

Thereafter, Dr. Kalam worked as the Chairman of the Technology, Information, Forecasting and Assessment Council (TIFAC).

Dr. Kalam played a significant role in India's Pokharan-II nuclear test that was conducted in 1998.

In November 1999, Dr. Kalam was appointed as the Chief Scientific Advisor to the Govt. of India.
Later, in November 2001 he Joined Anna University at Chennai as a Professor of Technology and Societal Transformation.

Dr. Kalam—A Great Leader

When Dr. Kalam was working at the Rocket launching station in Thumba, there were around 70 scientists working under his leadership. To get success in their work and plan the scientists used to work for 12 to 18 hours daily. They could hardly spare any time for their families.

One day, a scientist came to Dr. Kalam and said, "Sir, I've promised my kids to take them to the exhibition going on in the town. So, I want to leave at 5.30 pm today, if you permit."

Dr. Kalam accepted his request and permitted him to leave at 5.30 pm. The scientist got engaged in his work. But when he finished the work it was almost 8.00 pm. He felt very bad that he had broken the promise given to his kids. Dr. Kalam was not in the office at that time.

In a Sad and tired mood, when he reached home he saw that his children were not at home. He asked to his wife about them. She replied, "Your Boss came here around 5.00 pm and took our kids for the exhibition."

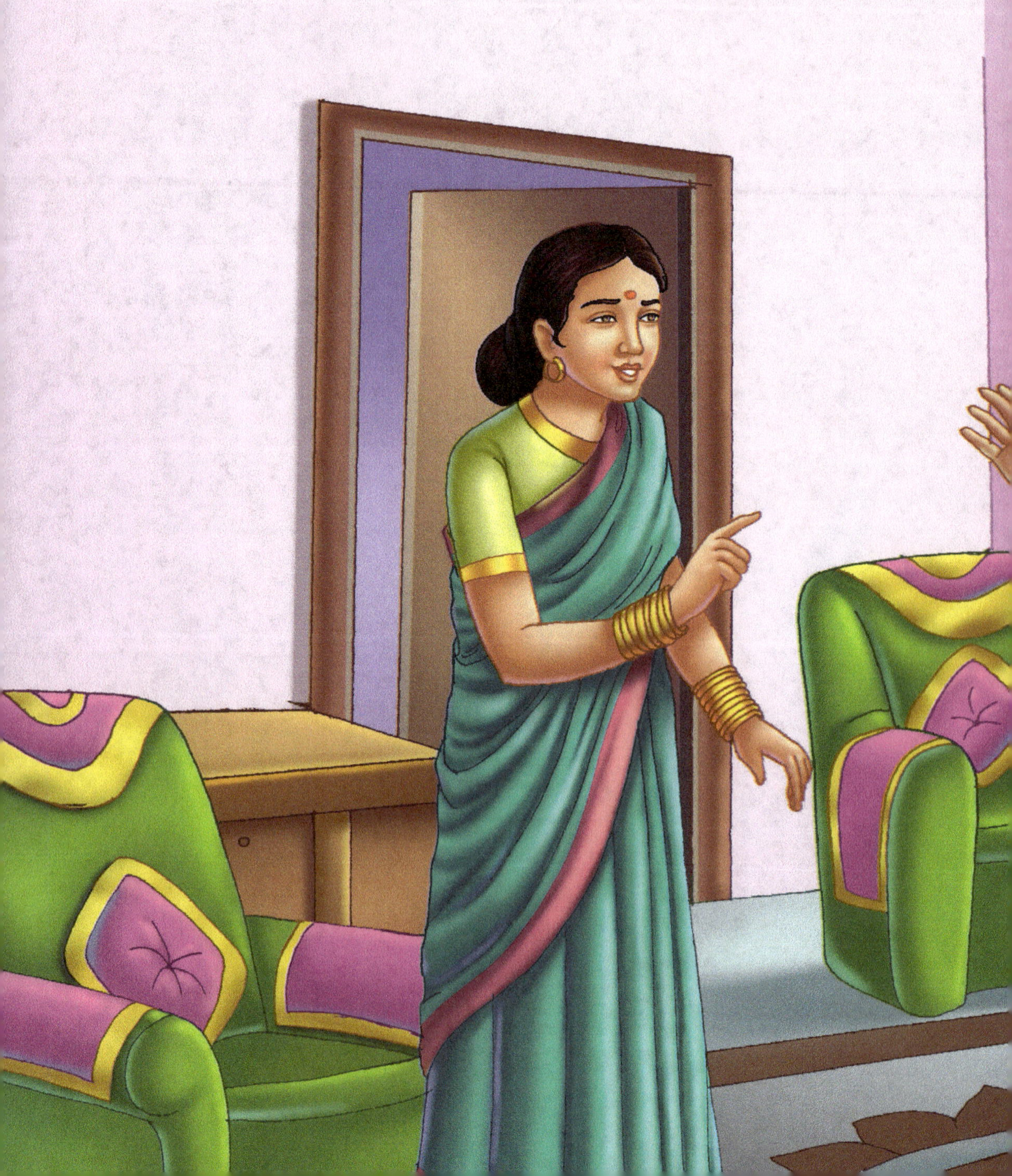

The scientist was overwhelmed by the sweet gesture of his boss. Actually, Dr. Kalam saw that the scientist was engrossed in a very important work. And, he didn't want to disappoint the kids. So, he decided to take his children on his behalf for the exhibition.

Such an understanding and caring boss was Dr. Kalam.

Dr. Kalam as the President of India

The entire nation was surprised when the ruling NDA Government nominated Dr. Kalam—the famous scientist—as their candidate for the President elections. He won the election by huge margin and became the 11th President of India on 25th July 2002.

In his speech during the oath taking ceremony, Dr. Kalam said that we should be proud of our country, "In the last 50 years, India has made many achievements in the fields of food production, health sector, higher education, media & mass communication, information technology, science and defence. In spite of these advancements, a large population is still struggling with the problems like poverty, unemployment, diseases and lack of education."

Dr. Kalam expressed his vision to eradicate all the problems from the country and making it the strongest nation one day.

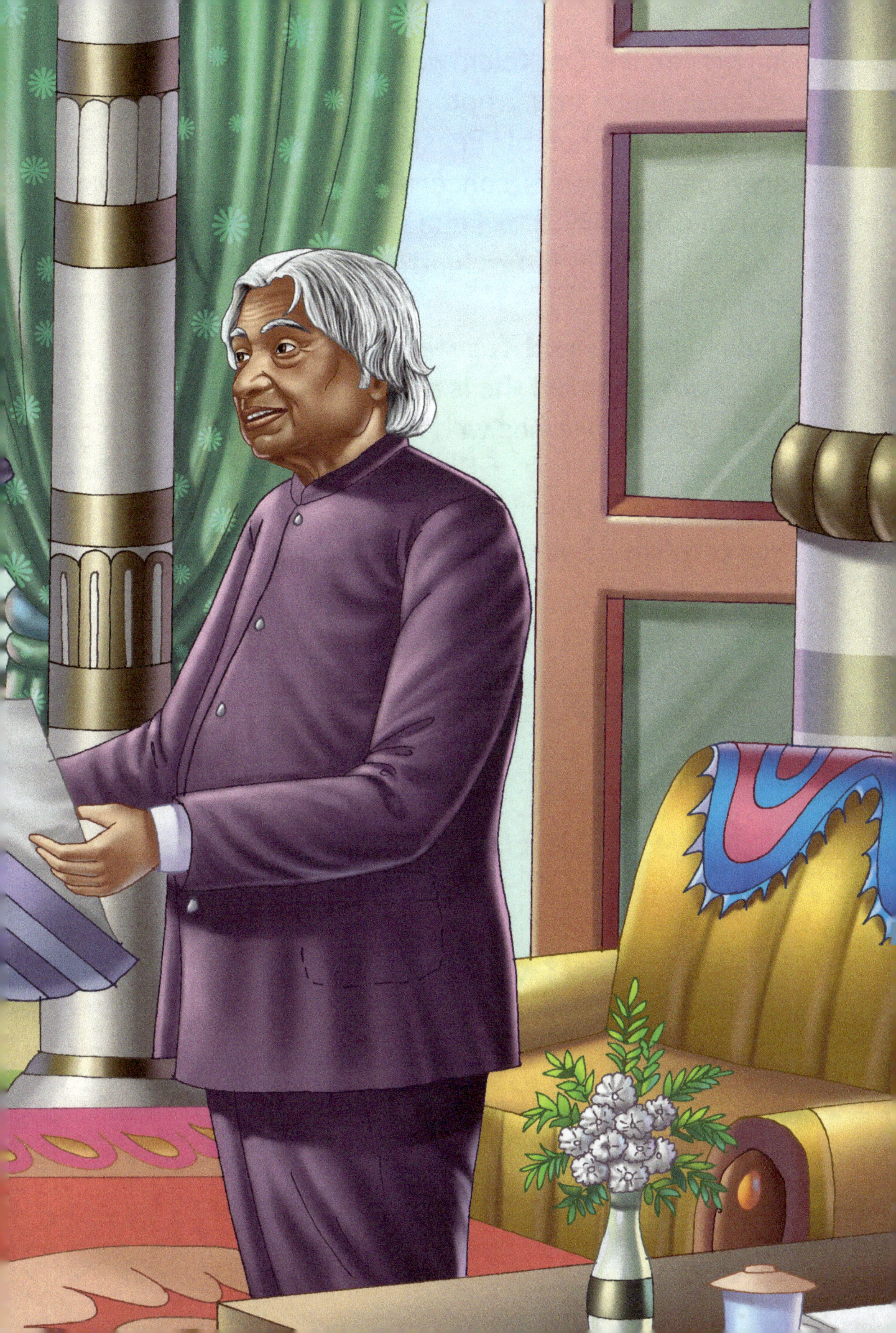

During his tenure, Dr. Kalam worked especially in the fields of science and education. He was remained as an approachable and humble President. He is very fond of the children and is always concerned for their development and welfare. He aimed to make India a scientifically strong nation and always tries to ignite the spark in the minds of Indian citizens.

Dr. Kalam has a multifaceted personality. Apart from being a great scientist, he is also interested in the field of arts and culture. He has written many books including his autobiography, 'Wings of Fire'. Some of his famous books are: 'Scientist to President', 'Ignited Minds: Unleashing the Power Within India', 'India 2020' etc.

He has also written Tamil poetry. Dr. Kalam is good at playing the Indian musical instrument 'Veena'.

Dr. Kalam has three visions. His first vision is freedom. He said that our country was ruled by many and remained dependent for a long period but we the Indians respect other's freedom, thus India has great values and culture.

Dr. Kalam's second vision is development. He said that though we have achieved a lot in the last few years, but we need to have more development, especially in the fields of education, science and technology.

His third vision is that India must be strong and emerge as a super power. It should stand up to the world and show its strength.

Dr. Kalam wants to make India an advanced and technologically developed nation. In his book, 'India 2020', he has mentioned an action plan to make India a knowledge superpower and a developed nation by the year 2020.

Dr. Kalam has been awarded with Bharat Ratna (1997), Padma Vibhushan (1990), Padma Bhushan (1981) and also received many more prestigious honours and awards.

He is presently the Chancellor of the Indian Institute of Space and Technology and also works as a professor at Anna University (Chennai) and as a visiting faculty in many academic and research institutes through out the country.

In May 2011, Dr. Kalam started a new mission for the Indian youth. 'What Can I Give Movement', is a unique mission to inculcate the Universal spirit of giving in the youth.

For years, Dr. Kalam has been inspiring many lives, especially the youth and children. He is the ocean of knowledge. We should draw inspiration from his life and must work to make India- a strongest nation.

On July 27, 2015, Dr. Kalam died after collapsing, while delivering a lecture at IIM, Shillong, Meghalaya. He was 83. The whole Nation mourned on his death, and paid homage, includes the President, the PM and other dignitaries, to him.

Birth and Early Years of Gurudev's Life

Rabindra Nath Tagore is one of the most popular and respected names in the field of Indian literature and music. Famous as Sobriquet Gurudev, he was a renowned poet, musician, writer, educationist, painter and social reformer.

Rabindra Nath Tagore was born in Kolkata (known as Calcutta earlier) in an affluent Bengali Brahmin family on 7th May 1861. He was the youngest of the thirteen children of his parents—Debendra Nath Tagore and Sharda Devi.

Since childhood, Rabindra Nath Tagore was inclined towards literature and music. He loved reading and spending time in library. At a very young age, he started reading the works of Kalidas and other famous Indian poets.

At the age of eight, Rabindra Nath Tagore wrote his first poetry. His parents were very proud to see his extraordinary skills and talent.

At the age of twelve, Rabindra Nath Tagore got an opportunity to visit many places of India with his father. He visited his father's Shantiniketan estate in Bholapur. And after that, he visited Punjab, Himachal Pradesh and Himalayas. This tour of India had a great impact on his young mind. He was fascinated to see the natural beauty and the rich culture of India.

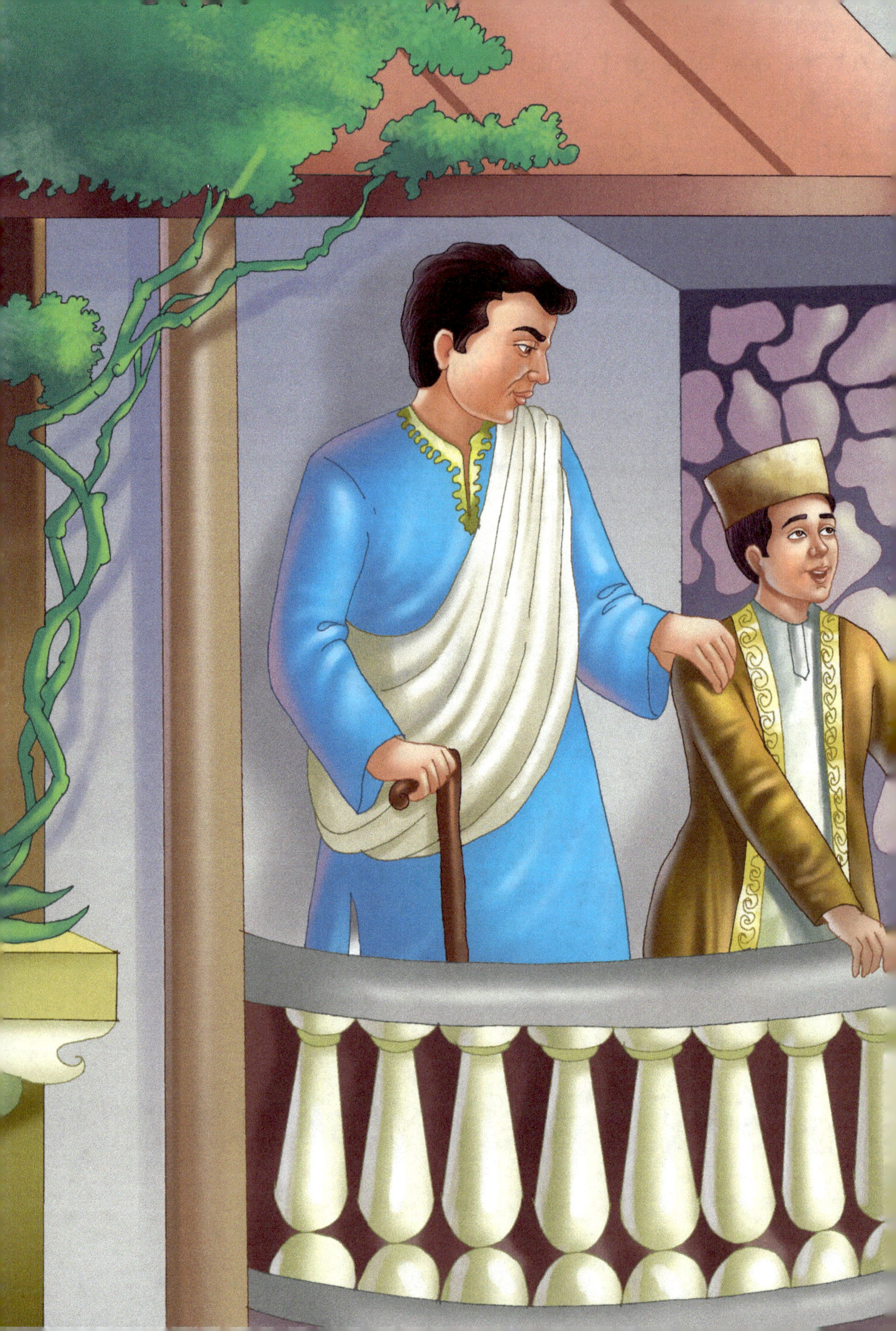

Rabindra Nath Tagore aspired to read more and more about Indian culture, nature and many more topics related to India. He was not much interested in his school studies. But his father wanted him to go out for higher studies to become a barrister.

Rabindra Nath Tagore's father bought a big house in Dalhousie—a place very close to the nature. Rabindra Nath Tagore was very happy to see the natural beauty of the place. Once, he expressed his love for nature and poetry to his father.

He said, "Baba, I just love to be in the lap of nature. I want to write about each and every beautiful thing of the nature."

"Yes. Dear Son, nature is full of the beauty and wonders. But I want you to concentrate more on your studies and become a barrister rather than wasting time in watching the sights and writing poems," replied Debendra Nath.

Debendra Nath was extremely worried to see Rabindra Nath's inclination towards the literature. He started planning to send him abroad for higher studies.

Rabindra Nath Tagore in Britain

In the year 1878, Rabindra Nath Tagore's father sent him to Britain for higher studies. He was only seventeen years old at that time. His elder brother Satyendra Nath was also with him.

Rabindra Nath got admission in a good school in London. After the school, he was admitted in the University of London. He was multitalented. He loved the new environment and learnt many new things in London. He was fond of the music.

He liked the western music a lot and soon learnt it nicely. Within a few months, he started composing wonderful songs and music.
Rabindra Nath was not serious for the higher studies. He could not complete his education and returned to India without completing degree.

Rabindra Nath's Return to India

In 1880, Debendra Nath called Rabindra Nath to come back to India. Rabindra Nath, on returning, pursued his interest in literature. He wrote a set of poetries and got it published for the first time. His work was hugely recognised and appreciated in Kolkata.

The admiration boosted Rabindra Nath's confidence to a great extent. He started devoting more and more time in reading and writing.

In 1884, Rabindra Nath experienced immense grief when his sister-in-law, Kadambari Devi, suddenly died. Rabindra Nath was very close to his sister-in-law. She was the one who took utmost care of him like her own child, after his mother's death.

This incident shattered Rabindra Nath. His sister-in-law was like a strong pillar in his life. She was also a friend and a mentor to him. She always encouraged him to pursue his love for literature and music.

Rabindra Nath decided to create something great and dedicate it to Kadambari Devi. He wrote a wonderful collection of verses named 'Bhanusimher Padavali', which proved to be a literary wonder at that time. He dedicated this great work to Kadambari Devi.

'Shaishav Sangeet' was his other creation that was dedicated to Kadambari Devi.

Great Works of Rabindra Nath Tagore

In the year 1883, Rabindra Nath got married to Bhavtarini Devi. After the marriage, she was given another name, Mrinalini Devi. Marriage brought a beautiful phase in Rabindra Nath's life. He lived very happily with his wife.

Rabindra Nath's passion for writing was continued to prosper even after his marriage. He gave great creative works one after the other. He also wrote some great plays.

All of his creations became very famous and were very much admired in the world of Indian Literature.

The life of villagers, and the lifestyle of Bengalees inspired Rabindra Nath to write short stories. His stories were also highly admired.

In the year 1891, Rabindra Nath had to shoulder his father's responsibilities of being a Zamindar. He took the charge of their family estates in Shelaidaha. He performed his duties of Zamindari with full dedication. And soon, he became the most lovable and respectfull name among the people. By this time, he was blessed with five children—two sons and three daughters.

In the year 1901, Rabindra Nath left Shelaidaha and moved to Bholapur Shantiniketan. There, he opened a school—Shantiniketan Brahmacharya Ashram. One of the first five students of this school was Bhavani Chandra Chaterjee. He was a great disciple of Rabindra Nath and he fondly called him, 'Gurudev.'

Soon, Rabindra Nath became popular by a sobriquet Gurudev. Shantiniketan was running successfully. But in 1902, his life was again clouded with the sorrows. His dear wife Mrinalini Devi died after a long illness. Rabindra Nath was completely broken. But soon, he got over from his grief and focused once again on his work.

At that time, India was under British Rule. Rabindra Nath Tagore was also concerned about India's freedom. He contributed in the freedom fight by writing inspirational poetries about India and the freedom fighters. 'Navedya' and 'Kheya' were his most popular patriotic writing. His speech, 'Swadesi Samaj' is still remembered. He also wrote many articles on freedom fights and the nation, which ignited the emotions of patriotism in his readers. Rabindra Nath once visited London with his son. During his journey, a great idea struck his mind. He thought, "How nice it would be to spread India's glory and rich culture in other countries also!"

This thought of Gurudev inspired him to create his literary masterpiece, 'Gitanjali'. In this masterpiece, he translated hundreds of his patriotic poetries in English. The great artist Rothenstein and the famous poet W. B. Yeats were impressed to see the Gurudev's poetry. W. B. Yeats wrote a beautiful introduction for Gitanjali.

On getting published in 1912, 'Gitanjali' created a wave of excitement in England. The People of England became great fans of Gurudev and his poetry.
Rabindra Nath Tagore was the first Indian to receive the Noble Prize, in the year 1913, for his outstanding contribution in literature.

After the achievement of Noble Prize, Gurudev was also honoured by the prestigious title of 'Sir' by the British Government. This is the first time any Indian was offered a knighthood.

Apart from his contribution in the literature, he also gifted a unique form of the music called Rabindra Sangeet to the Indian society.

There was no field of art that remained untouched by multitalented Gurudev. He also created marvellous paintings and sketches. Many exhibitions were held to display his great work.

Rabindra Nath was also a social worker. He tried to eradicate many ill social practises and issues. He also worked and spread awareness to end the culture of 'Untouchability'.
During his lifetime, Gurudev met many famous personalities like Einstein, Mussolini and H. G. Wells.

Gurudev wrote a large number of poems, stories, articles, speeches and songs in his lifetime.

During the last years of his life, he also wrote his autobiography.

The Indian national anthem, 'Jana gana mana', was also written by Rabindra Nath Tagore.

The Last Phase of Gurudev's Life

The pace of Gurudev's work did not slow down irrespective of his old age. He continued writing, reading, delivering lectures, social services and visiting foreign countries. His excessive involvement in work affected his body badly. His health started deteriorating day by day.

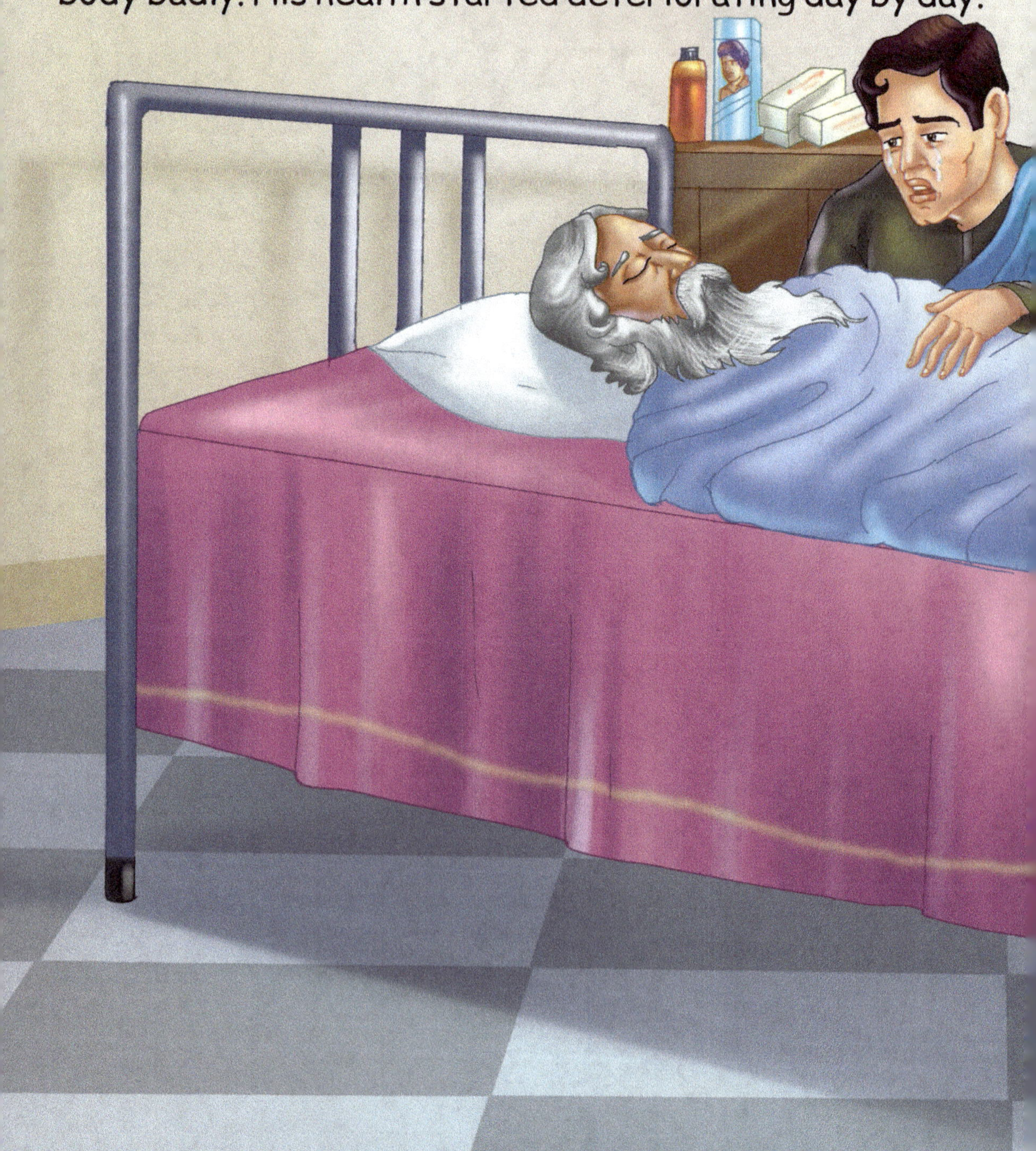

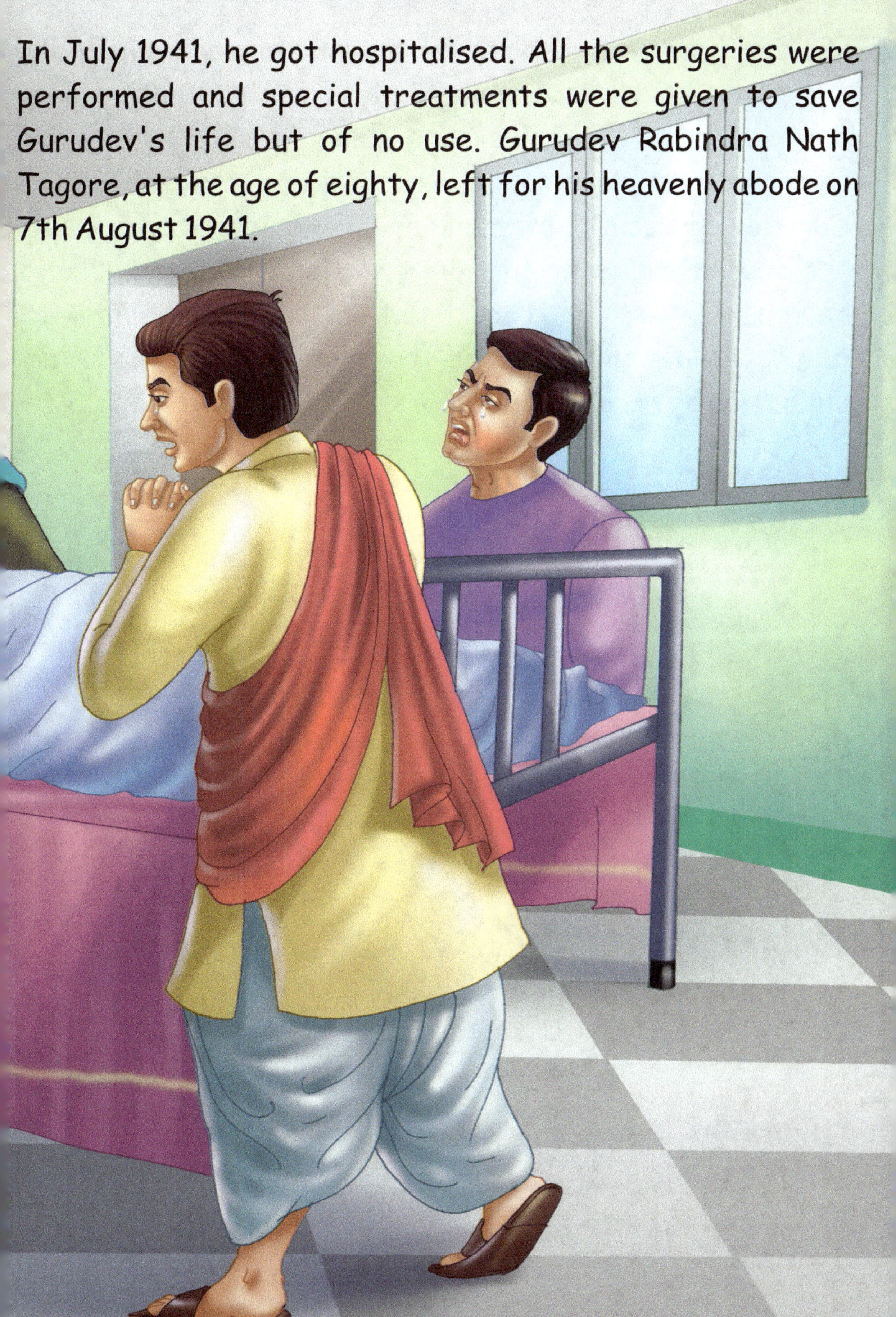

In July 1941, he got hospitalised. All the surgeries were performed and special treatments were given to save Gurudev's life but of no use. Gurudev Rabindra Nath Tagore, at the age of eighty, left for his heavenly abode on 7th August 1941.

His death was a big shock for millions of people in India and abroad. It was a very big loss for our nation. His poetries, dramas, stories, songs and music are still fondly remembered through out the country and also in abroad. Gurudev spread the message of love, unity, brotherhood and peace through his literary creations. We should learn and draw inspiration from the life of this great man, who dedicated his entire life in transforming and improving our nation by his incredible work.

www.ingramcontent.com/pod-product-compliance
Lightning Source LLC
LaVergne TN
LVHW080601200726
843510LV00004B/978